Betsy Potter thinks boys have everything their own way and she's not going to put up with it any longer. Software understands just what she means. After all, don't snails have everything *their* own way? But when Betsy gets hold of her brother Tom's computer, she puts herself and Software (who's watching) into a computer stupor — and they both start behaving very oddly indeed. While Betsy is walking around like a zombie causing trouble for her dad at school, Software has banned squiggling and is forcing the snails to move in straight lines. And he's got two large and ugly bully snail bodyguards to make sure they do! Things are looking very black for the snail colony until User-Friendly comes up with a brilliant plan to get Software back to normal.

By the same author:

Software Superslug

Software Superslug

and

The Great Computer Stupor

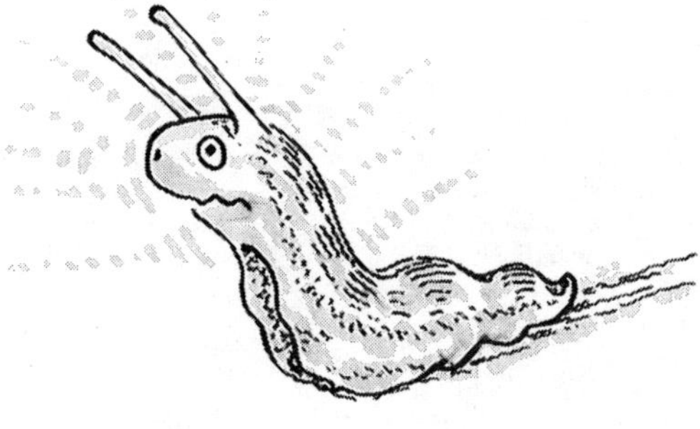

Joyce Dunbar

Illustrated by James Dunbar

Macdonald Children's Books

First published in Great Britain in 1989
by Macdonald Children's Books

Photoset in 13pt Baskerville by Leaper & Gard Ltd
Printed and bound in Great Britain by
The Guernsey Press Co. Ltd, Guernsey, Channel Islands

Macdonald Children's Books
Simon and Schuster International Group
Wolsey House, Wolsey Road
Hemel Hempstead HP2 4SS

BRITISH LIBRARY CATALOGUING IN PUBLICATION DATA
Dunbar, Joyce.
Software superslug and the great computer stupor.
I. Title II. Dunbar, James
823'.914 [J]

ISBN 0-356-16777-1
ISBN 0-356-16778-X Pbk

Contents

Chapter 1

"It's a Thunderbolt!"

A snail called User-Friendly was fast asleep in his shell. Around him, in a brick-built hole next to the cellar, were lots of other snails, also sound asleep.

Daylight peeped into the hole all round the rim at the top, but this didn't bother the snails.

Footsteps scrunched on the gravel, but the sound didn't bother the snails. They snored and bubbled and dreamed.

But suddenly there was a different noise. Something smacked sharply on to the gravel, slid down the side of the hole, and landed with a clatter in their midst.

This *did* bother the snails.

Slowly, as snails do, they poked their tentacles

out of their shells to see what had fallen amongst them.

It was long, and straight, and shiny, and covered with strange black markings. It leaned upright against the wall and kept very, very still.

"What is it?" said User-Friendly, who was the chief snail.

"Is it alive?" said Cat-Flap, who was a fat round grandma snail.

"Can you eat it?" said Slipper-Sock, who was always thinking of food.

Curiosity got the better of the snails, and they cautiously gathered round to examine the object more closely. It was like a stick of solid slime, pressed out flat and straight.

"It smells new," said Fast-Forward, with a disappointed sniff.

"You can see through it," said Whizz-Kid.

"It's a thunderbolt!" said Floppy-Disc, who had been sleeping near the spot where it landed and was still in a state of shock.

"No it's not," said User-Friendly. "I don't think it's hostile. But then again, it isn't exactly *friendly*."

"It's not *us*, not our sort of thing," agreed Cat-Flap.

Mostly the snails welcomed the mix of rubbish that floated off the street and on to the drive, eventually drifting down into The Hole where they lived – sweet wrappers, crisp packets, old cartons, bottle tops, dead leaves and the like. When it was all bedded down with the dirt and cobwebs, it made the place very snug.

But this thing would never be snug. It would never bed down with anything. It was much too cold and hard.

"We must ask Software what it is," said User-Friendly. "With that amazing brain of his, he's sure to be able to tell."

"Where is Software?" asked Floppy-Disc.

"I think he's sulking," answered Cat-Flap. "The last time I saw him he was complaining that he didn't want to be software. He said he'd sooner have a shell and be hardware. He says nobody loves a slug."

"But he's a SUPERSLUG!" said Whizz-Kid.

"He says that makes things worse," said Cat-Flap. "He says that nobody loves a superslug even more than they don't love a slug."

"There's no pleasing some slugs," said Whizz-Kid impatiently. "How many times must we tell him he's a genius? How many times must we thank him for finding us The Hole to live in, for giving us our wonderful names? We can't sing his praises all the time. Let him sulk!"

"Let who sulk?" said a voice.

It was Software, coming through the air vent, which was the back entrance to The Hole, leading from the cellar of the Potter family house.

Unlike the snails, Software didn't need much sleep. It was because of his highly active brain. It was an anything-but-sluggish brain. While the

snails snoozed away the daylight hours, Software would prowl around the house, thinking, wondering, exploring.

That's what he'd just been doing and now he had returned to find the snails all wide awake and this very strange object in their midst.

Chapter 2

"OOOOGHAAAA!"

"Look what's fallen into The Hole, Software," said User-Friendly. "What do you think it is?"

Software looked at the object. Even if he knew what it was, he obviously wasn't telling – for what Cat-Flap had said was true.

Software was in a sulk.

You see, although he was so clever, he also had a bit of a problem. He thought he was a snail without a shell. He would often mutter under his breath about what he called the 'withs' and 'withouts'. Even in his dreams he had been heard to call out, "A shell! A shell! My genius for a shell!"

It was only because of his genius that the snails

put up with him at all. You see, he understood human talk – which made him the perfect spy. The information he picked up! The tittle-tattle he passed on! The sheer and wondrous knowledge! Without the help of Software, the snails wouldn't know a booze-up from a booby-trap!

Software was good at booze-ups (but that's another story). He was good at finding food. He was good at places to live. He was absolutely brilliant at names. Added up, it made him almost good enough for snails, but alas, not good enough for himself.

For he knew, in his heart of hearts, what snails think about slugs: 'OOOOGHAAAA!'

He knew what humans think about slugs: an even bigger 'OOOOOOGHAAAAAA!'

And though he didn't like to admit it, he thought the same about slugs himself: 'OOOOGHAAAA!'

The snails could tell what sort of mood he was in and that it was best to leave him alone. The light was beginning to fade and they decided to set off for their usual nightly feasting in the garden.

"Are you coming Software?" asked Cat-Flap, who really did have a soft spot for him, but as Software didn't answer, the snails set off on their own.

Software watched them go, crawling slowly up the sides of The Hole, leaving wriggly trails of slime. He tried not to notice the way their shells tilted elegantly from side to side as they moved, and their different beautiful patterns.

It really wasn't fair!

When at last they were gone, Software breathed a sigh of relief. He liked to be alone in The Hole. Though he said so himself, it was the perfect place for snails; warm and damp and muggy, with a front entrance into the garden and a back entrance into the cellar. A stone sink over the top, full of plants, kept it hidden from prying eyes. They called it 'Hole Sweet Hole'.

But he was pleased to see them go for another reason. Although he had tried not to show it, his curiosity was greatly aroused by the object that had fallen in, and he was eager to investigate.

He had seen something like it before on Mr Potter's desk. It had the same sort of marks and numbers, the same sheer straight edges; but Mr Potter's was made of wood, whereas this one was transparent plastic.

Software knew what it was of course: it was a ruler. He also knew that Mr Potter was a schoolteacher, who thought rulers very important. But why? What was it for? And what was it doing in The Hole?

In a slanting shaft of moonlight, the edges of the ruler gleamed. So did all the slime trails on the wall. Software couldn't help but notice the difference.

The sides of the ruler were neat and straight – beautifully neat and straight!

The slime trails, on the other hand, scribbled all over the place, like wriggly, squiggly mazes.

"Perhaps," thought Software, "the ruler is some

sort of message. Perhaps it is to teach us a lesson. Perhaps we should learn to crawl straight!"

He rather liked the idea. He felt he'd be good at straight lines. His shape, after all, was much sleeker, more streamlined than any snail's. He decided to give it a try.

As steadily and straight as he could, he began to crawl up the ruler. He fell off once or twice and had to start again. He wandered off course and found he had criss-crossed from the front of the ruler to the back. Following the edge of a ruler wasn't as easy as it looked!

But in the end he made it. He had just completed one whole length when he heard a gurgling and gasping and hiccuping. It was the snails returning from the garden.

"That's funny," thought Software. "It's nowhere near daylight yet."

User-Friendly appeared first, obviously in a tearing hurry.

"Software! You should have seen them!" he gasped.

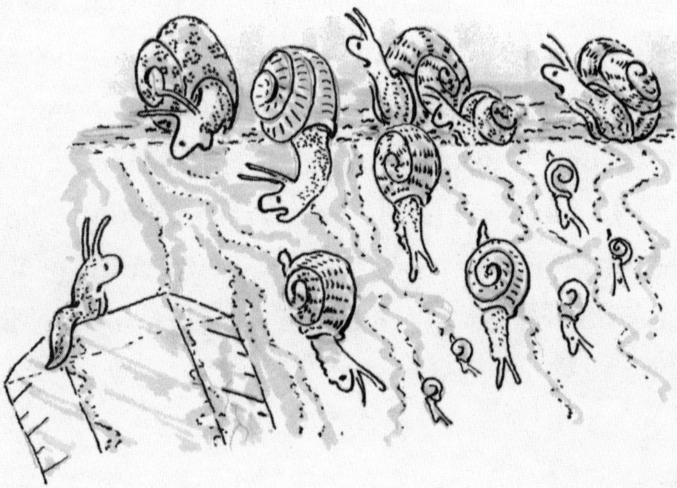

"They had great big scaly faces!" said Whizz-Kid, following closely behind.

"And shells as hard as nails!" added Floppy-Disc, who came next.

By now the rest of the snails had appeared, swarming, slithering, scrambling down the sides of The Hole in their efforts to get to the bottom.

Then the snails told Software about the two great snails that had gate-crashed from a neighbouring garden and grabbed the best bits of food.

"They pinched my tulip shoot!" said Slipper-Sock indignantly.

"And they threatened to follow us home!" said Whizz-Kid. "You should have seen them move! They said their great-great grandmother was a champion racing snail!"

"But we managed to give them the slip," said Whole-Meal. "Aren't we clever?"

"Not nearly as clever as me," said Software, from the very tip-top of the ruler. "Watch this!"

Chapter 3

Gate-Crashers

When he was sure that each snail had a view, Software crawled down the side of the ruler in a stately and dignified manner.

"There!" he said proudly when he had reached the bottom. "How about that?"

The snails were totally baffled.

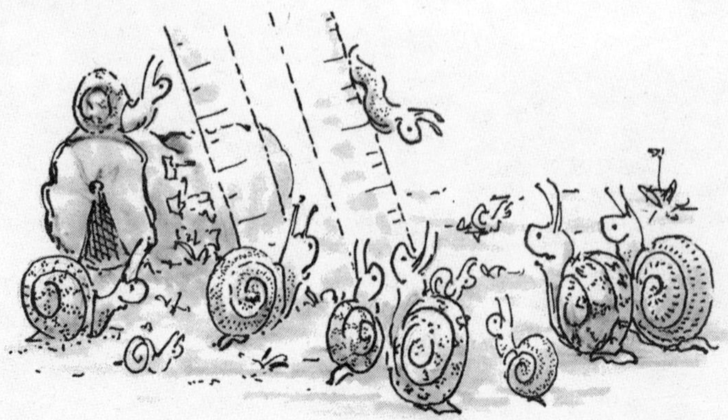

"Software," said User-Friendly, "I'm sorry to have to tell you but –"

"But what?" snapped Software.

"Any old snail could do that."

"Come on then, let's see you," Software challenged.

"I shouldn't if I were you," said Cat-Flap. "It might bite."

"Anything a slug can do, I can do better," bragged User-Friendly, having first go. It was hopeless. He wobbled and swayed about, unable to keep his balance.

"All I need is a bit of practice," he said sheepishly.

"All we need is a bit of practice," said the rest of the snails, as they charged together for the ruler.

After the fright they'd had in the garden, the snails were in the mood for some fun. Soon the ruler was smothered in snails, like barnacles on the bottom of a boat. They tumbled and toppled about, until their weight brought the ruler crashing down across the side of an old tin can.

"Oops-a-daisy," they chortled.

"You've missed the whole point!" scolded Software, as the snails made the interesting discovery that the ruler was now a snail see-saw.

Software sat in the middle, trying to assert himself.

"Don't you see," he hectored, "that I crawled in a dead straight line! You could learn to do the same!"

"Why should we want to do that?" asked Slipper-Sock, slowly rising into the air.

"To get around faster for a start," said Software.

"But why should we want to do that?" asked Slipper-Sock, by now on a downward turn.

"Lots of reasons!" said Software. "To save slime – I mean – time."

"But why should we want to save time?" asked Floppy-Disc. "What for?"

"Don't you want to get ahead?" snapped Software, furious with the snails for being so stupid.

"I've already got a head," said Whole-Meal. "What would I do with two?"

No sooner had he said these words than two terrible heads appeared at the top of The Hole.

The snails went still and quiet.

Gliding smoothly down the side of The Hole came two enormous snails. They had squashed-in, scaly faces and hard, tough looking shells. It was the gate-crashers from the garden, obviously looking for trouble.

They steam-rollered straight towards Software, pushing the other snails off the ruler and approaching from either side.

"Ugh! A slimy slug! A 'orrible little slug!" they sneered. "We knows just what to do wiv slugs. We squeezes 'em till they bubbles and squeaks."

Software was too frightened to move.

While the snails looked on in horror they shouldered Software between them and started to lean on him hard.

"Help me somebody!" pleaded Software. "Whizz-Kid! Slipper-Sock! Help!"

But the snails had gone into their shells, just too squeamish to watch.

Software squashed himself flat, so that the bullies came face to scaly face.

"Did you 'ear what 'e called you?" said one to the other. "'E called you Fizzy-Wig."

"And did you 'ear what 'e called you?" replied the other. "'E called you Sloppy-Sick!"

Software was about to be crushed when Cat-Flap found the courage to speak, just peeping out of her shell.

"He wasn't calling you names. Those are our names!"

Seizing his chance, Software dived into the tin can, out through a rusty hole, under the mat of dead leaves, and squeezed into a crack in the wall.

"Come on out of there you squidgy little squirt!" snarled the snails, steaming with bad temper.

But Software knew he was safe, at least for the time being. Being a slug had its good points after all.

Chapter 4

Girls, Boys and Bellyfoots

Although the bullies threatened to starve him out, Software could tell from their snoring that by morning they were fast asleep.

Creeping out of the crack, he slithered over their backs (which were much too thick for them to feel through) and crawled to the top of The Hole. A little way further under the stone sink and he was soon on the gravelled path.

Suddenly the front door opened. It was Mrs Potter in her dressing gown, collecting the eggs and milk. Software dived for safety under the nearest object – which was the carton full of eggs. On its underside were a couple of hollows. He hid himself tightly inside one.

Hardly a moment later he was whisked into the house and placed on the breakfast table.

"Anyone for boiled eggs?" sang out Mrs Potter.

"Crikey!" thought Software. "Talk about out of

the frying pan into the fire! It'll be anyone for boiled slugs next!" He raced round beneath the edge of a plate to the underside of the kitchen table where it seemed safe enough to stay put.

So it was that Software heard every word of the conversation between the Potter family over breakfast.

"Have you tidied your room Betsy?" said Mrs Potter. "It was an absolute glory-hole last night."

"Why me?" said Betsy. "What about Tom's room? It's worse than mine. Boys can be as untidy as they like. It's not fair!"

Tom was reading from his wildlife magazine that had come with the paper that morning. "Listen. It says here that slugs and snails are called bellyfoots!"

"Do you mind," groaned Betsy. "I'm having my breakfast."

"Tell me more," said Mrs Potter enthusiastically.

Ever since the discovery that they had a slug genius on the premises, Mrs Potter had taken a keen interest in slugs and snails. It was Software's slime trails that had given the game away. She kept a record of them and there was no doubt about it: his was *intelligent* slime; his was *artistic* slime. It was slime with a sense of purpose, not slime that went anyhow, anywhere. It was a mystery that fascinated Mrs Potter and which she wanted to unravel.

"Well it's really gastropod," explained Tom. " 'Gastro' means belly and –"

"– 'pod' means foot!" concluded Mrs Potter.

"That's right!" said Tom. "Their belly is also their foot! Just think of that!"

"I'd rather not," protested Betsy.

"So anyone who studies their behaviour is called a gastropodologist," said Mrs Potter knowingly.

"Bellyfootologist," joked Tom. "That's what you are Mum!"

Mr Potter lowered his newspaper. "What's that?" he said. "Are you calling your mother rude names?"

All eyes turned to Mr Potter. He was looking very strange. His hair was unusually flattened. His tie was unusually straight. He looked as if he'd been laid out on the ironing board and pressed.

"Is anything the matter dear?" asked Mrs Potter . . . and then she suddenly remembered.

"Oooh! Today's the day isn't it?" she said, buttering a bit more toast.

"So it is!" said Betsy and Tom brightly. They already knew that Mr Scroggles, their headmaster, was away for a week on a course and that their father had been left in charge. Of course, they felt that a man who had ticklish feet and kept his old teddy bear by the bed couldn't possibly be a *real* headmaster. Tom was looking forward to some fun.

"Can we play football all afternoon?" he asked his father. "Can we have an hour for break?"

Betsy's eyes gleamed at this, but she didn't say a word. *She* had plans of her own.

"Not a bit of it my lad," said Mr Potter. "A headmaster has a big responsibility and I expect you two to set an example. Tom, clean your teeth! Betsy, comb your hair! Tom, your school bag's covered in stickers. Betsy, your shoes need a polish!"

Betsy and Tom looked at each other in dismay. It was embarrassing enough for them to have their father teaching in the same school, but oh dear! If he carried on like this! It would be 'Potter the Rotter' instead of 'Dotty Potter'. Perhaps he was putting it on. Perhaps the best thing to do was play along with him for now.

"Has anyone seen my new ruler?" said Tom, stuffing things into his school bag.

"It must be where you put it," said his mother. "Rulers don't just get up and walk."

Software had seen the ruler of course, but was thinking deeply about his bellyfoot. By the time Mrs Potter had seen the family off to school, he had thought himself deeply to sleep.

Chapter 5

Sexism and Slugism

It was tea-time when Software woke up. Betsy and Tom were sitting at the table while Mrs Potter poured out the tea.

"Your father's late," she said. "How did it go today?"

"*Awful*!" protested Betsy. "We'll *never* live it down. We get teased enough as it is."

"Awful? Why? What happened?"

"It was *Dad*!" joined in Tom. "He really laid it on. At first we thought he was joking, but then –"

"What then?"

"He just went on and on," continued Betsy. "Like a cardboard cut-out headmaster! Like something from a pop-up book!"

"I heard that!" said Mr Potter, bursting into the room and slumping into a chair. He looked cross and rather crumpled.

"Have a cup of tea dear," said Mrs Potter.

Mr Potter ignored her and went on talking to Betsy. "As for that petition of yours! Here am I, acting headmaster for a week –"

"*Over*-acting headmaster," muttered Tom.

"And what does my daughter do? My very own daughter? She presents me with a PETITION, in front of the whole school!"

"Petition?" queried Mrs Potter.

"That's right!" said Betsy indignantly. "They told us we were all going to do CDT –"

"CDT?" said a puzzled Mrs Potter.

"Craft Design Technology!" answered Betsy.

"That sounds very impressive".

"That's what I thought!" said Betsy scornfully. But do you know what it turned out to be? Woodwork as usual for the boys! Needlework as usual for the girls.

"You won't catch me doing needlework!" scoffed Tom. "And *you* wouldn't know one end of a hammer from the other."

"Nor one end of an idiot from the other!" retorted Betsy. "Girls are just as good as boys. They can do things just as well. They can do some things a whole lot better!"

"Stop that!" bawled Mr Potter. "If you feel so strongly about it, why didn't you present your petition to Mr Scroggles?"

"Because he wouldn't have taken any notice!" said Betsy. "You know how old fashioned he is. The school is old fashioned. In all the other schools around here the girls can even wear trousers!"

"And can the boys wear skirts?" snorted Tom.

"Oh you!" said Betsy. "You and your ideas about girls! Boys have things all their own way! You're sexist! That's what you are! And so are you Dad! I thought you'd be *pleased* about our petition. I thought –"

"Hey Dad, we're sexy," hooted Tom.

"See! A boy! A stupid boy!" yelled Betsy, throwing a bread roll at her brother.

"BETSY! THAT'S ENOUGH! GO TO YOUR ROOM!" shouted Mr Potter. "AND TIDY IT UP WHEN YOU GET THERE!"

Betsy stormed out of the room. There was silence for a while, then Mrs Potter quietly said, "Well I do think she's got a point."

"SO DO I," thought Software from under the table. "She's got lots and lots of points!"

He'd been taking it all in and his mind was in a fast spin.

"It's just the same for slugs! Snails have things all their own way! And why? Slugs are just as good as snails! They can do things just as well! They can do some things a whole lot better! They're sleeker, smoother, more streamlined. They can crawl in much straighter lines! They can squeeze into much smaller spaces! Slugs are ... well ... *subtle.* Snails are so ... so ... OBVIOUS!"

The more he thought about it, the more it all made sense. For no good reason he could see, slugs were a downtrodden lot.

"Of all the creatures in the world, the most unloved is a slug! The most despised is a slug! Slugs are the lowest of the low! Slugism! That's what it is!"

He puffed out his chest with pride as he made a

final declaration. "But I, Software Superslug, am going to change all that!"

All this was to himself of course, which seemed a waste of very fine words. He longed to climb from beneath the table to the top of the butter dish and make a speech to the Potter family. But he thought he'd better not in case they decided to boil him. Besides, Betsy wasn't there to hear.

He would try it out first on the snails.

Chapter 6

The Naming of Snails

While Mrs Potter cleared away the tea things, Software set off back to The Hole.

He had just reached the bottom of the table leg when he saw Floppy-Disc and Fast-Forward crawling down the side of the door jamb, looking extremely obvious.

He was very surprised. He'd never known the snails enter the house before while the family were up and about. He joined them both in the hall.

"Software! Where have you been? We've been looking everywhere for you," began Fast-Forward. "Something terrible –"

"I've got news! Wonderful news!" interrupted Software. "You've got it all wrong about slugs! They're not the nasty, filthy, dirty, horrible, revolting creatures you always thought they were. Slugs are really very nice!"

"What *are* you on about Software?" asked Floppy-Disc.

It was only then that Software noticed how worried the two snails looked. "Slugs are really . . .

quite . . . nice," he faltered, looking anxiously from one to the other.

"Never mind that!" snapped Fast-Forward, "Don't you realize we've got a crisis on our hands?"

"Crisis? What crisis?" said Software.

"They've pushed us out of The Hole," said Floppy-Disc. "Bulldozed us into the cellar."

"Who? What?" said Software, then he remembered. In the excitement of his new ideas he'd forgotten the two intruders. Now, as Floppy-Disc explained, it all came back to him.

"They're claiming squatters' rights, and there's nothing we can do about it, because they've got Cat-Flap in there. She just won't come out of her shell. Unless we do as they say, they've threatened to roll her to the top of The Hole and drop her so that she breaks."

"Ugh," Software shuddered.

"And they won't let us into the garden," went on Floppy-Disc, "which means we won't get anything to eat."

"But what can I do about it?" said Software.

"I'm only a slug you know, a poor, weak, under-privileged slug."

"Oh come off it Software!" said Floppy-Disc. "You know very well what a clever slug you are. You can think of something."

"They won't go because of that straight thing," said Fast-Forward. "They say it's an exercise track for the training of racing snails."

"Really?" said Software, and then a thought struck him. "What are they called?"

"Oh they haven't got names!" answered Floppy-Disc. "They don't bother with things like that . . ."

"Then I'll give them some names!" exclaimed Software. "You know what they say – 'Give a snail a nice name . . .' Snails are like everything else.

They begin to *look* like their names. After a while they even *behave* like their names."

"In that case, how about Posy and Blossom?" said Fast-Forward. "It might make them sweeter."

"Or Gurgles and Bubbles," suggested Floppy-Disc. "It might make them softer."

They crawled under the cellar door on to the cold stone steps, with Software thinking hard all the way.

"Cheesecake and Cracker-Jack?" he said grimly. "Squatter and Squeegee?"

It was no good. The naming of snails is a difficult matter, and Software just wasn't inspired.

"It won't work anyway," he said despondently. "It will take much more than names to shift those two."

"Software –" began Floppy-Disc, but before he had time to say more there were shouts on the landing up above that echoed all round the cellar, setting all the cobwebs shivering and sending the snails into their shells.

"Don't worry, I'll think of a way –" said Software, going off to see what was the matter.

It was a row between Betsy and Tom.

Chapter 7

Shoot the Squigglies

"Well, why shouldn't I borrow it?" said Betsy.

"Because it's MINE," yelled Tom. "You've got a doll's house, remember?"

"You can borrow my doll's house then," said Betsy.

"I don't want your stupid doll's house!"

"Stupid! Who are you calling stupid?"

Mrs Potter had heard them too and went hurrying up the stairs.

Through a crack in the staircase panelling Software saw Betsy and Tom on the landing squabbling over Tom's computer.

"What is it now?" said Mrs Potter wearily.

"It's Betsy!" howled Tom. "She's taken my map

of the world off the wall and swapped it for a mouse's tea-party poster! And now she's trying to pinch my computer!"

"I only want to borrow it," yelled Betsy. "Why should Tom have a computer and not me? It's just the same at school. The girls can't get near the computer because the boys hog it all the time."

By now Mr Potter had joined them. He sighed, Betsy did have a point.

"Can't she borrow it for this evening?" he said.

"Have you seen her room?" answered Tom. "It's a tip! She's got nowhere to put a computer. She doesn't know how to use it! It's delicate! It's complicated! She'll mess it up! She's just a stupid girl."

Finally, after much moaning and groaning from Tom, and arguing and persuading from his parents, it was decided that Betsy and Tom should swap rooms for the night so that Betsy could have a go on the computer. Betsy kept gleefully silent.

Software listened with interest. There was nothing he liked better than computer games, and it didn't much matter to him who was at the controls. Also, it was just possible that it would inspire him to think of the right names for the gate-crashers.

He waited until all was calm and then crept slowly into Tom's room. Betsy stared at the computer screen, her face flickering weirdly in its on-off, on-off glow. She was playing a game of 'SHOOT THE SQUIGGLIES'. From a plastic dinosaur on a shelf, Software made sure he had a view.

There was a shrill, high-pitched whine and green squigglies appeared on the screen.

Betsy shot one down with her missile, which went in a dead straight line.

ZOOOOOOOOOOOOOOOOOOOOOM!

straight to its target.

ZAP! a green squiggly was destroyed.

The whining began again, the sound rising and falling, while Betsy shot two more:

Whiiiiiiiine Whiiiiiiiiiine Whiiiiiiiiine Whiiiiiiiine

ZOOOOOOOOOOOOOOOOOOOM!

ZAP!

ZOOOOOOOOOOOOOOOOOOOM!

ZAP!

Betsy's eyes grew wide and her body tensed with excitement. Software was absolutely spellbound. More squigglies swarmed into view. Betsy zapped them down until a notice appeared on the screen:

```
Squigglies destroyed - 18
Well done. You win this time.
Now prepare for our next attack.
```

There was no stopping Betsy after that. The more games she won, the more she wanted to play. The more she played, the more green squigglies she destroyed.

ZOOOOOOOOOOOOOOOOOOOM!

ZAP!

ZOOOOOOOOOOOOOOOOOOOM!

ZAP!

– with her score getting higher and higher, until

she suddenly burst into tears. "Poor poor squigglies," she sobbed. "I've shot so many squigglies." Software sobbed too, in sympathy, though he wasn't sure who for.

Betsy tried to switch off the machine. But she couldn't! Her hands wouldn't do as she told them! She couldn't find the switch-off button! The machine whined and zoomed and zapped.

Betsy was too far gone. Like Software, she was well and truly programmed, to think as the computer thought, to do as the computer wanted. And it wanted to be kept switched on . . .

. . . and on

. . . and on

until both Betsy and Software were in a computer stupor.

Chapter 8

The Great Computer Stupor

"Where *is* he?" the snails were saying to each other, down in the darkness of the cellar.

"He said he would find a way –" said Floppy Disc.

"But *when*? *Where*? *How*? *What*?" they kept asking.

They were very, very hungry. All they'd had to eat that night were the remains of a mouldy apple and a few mince-pie crumbs they'd found in a box full of Christmas decorations. Slipper-Sock still rummaged around, all tangled up in some tinsel, hoping to find some more.

"Don't worry," User-Friendly reassured them. "Software would never let us down."

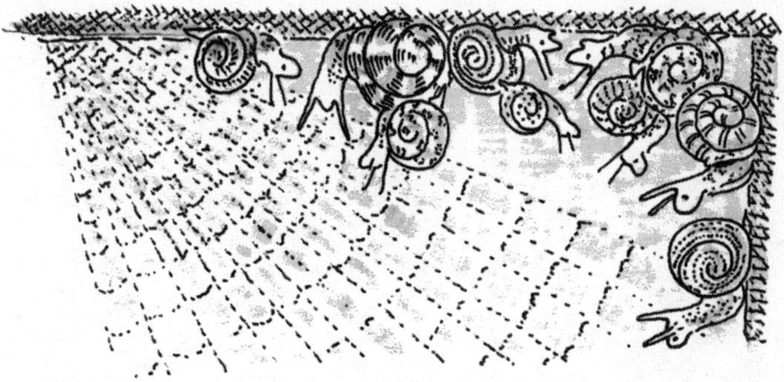

From the ceiling rafter of the cellar, where they huddled together amongst the cobwebs, they could see into The Hole. The bully boys were still in charge. They strolled around like armoured tanks, hard, grey, steely. Still as a stone was Cat-Flap, shut tight inside her shell.

"Oh I do wish he'd hurry up," said Whizz-kid nervously.

Then, through a crack in the staircase panelling, a small creature appeared. In straight lines it moved towards them, sharply turning corners at an angle.

"Something's coming!" said Whizz-Kid.

"What is it?" said Whole-Meal.

"It looks like a clockwork slug," said Floppy-Disc.

"A sleep-creeping slug," said Fast-Forward.

"Why no, it's Software," murmured User-Friendly. "What's the matter Software? You look as if you've had a funny turn."

"Don't you mention any sort of turn to me," rattled Software. "One squiggle and you're dead!"

"Huh? What?" said the mightily puzzled snails.

"They're going to shoot all the squigglies," Software snapped.

"Stop talking gibberish," said Fast-Forward, "and tell us if you thought of some names."

"This isn't the time for another of your daft ideas," User-Friendly joined in. "We've got those two blighters in there to get rid of."

"Might you be meaning us?" snarled a voice from inside The Hole. It was one of the bully-boy snails.

"It's that 'orrible little slug," said the other, "come back to get squashed after all."

Software ignored this remark, but in a spluttering spasm of outrage, turned on the rest of the snails, "You wriggly, squiggly, rabble of snails! You slimy, grimy, gastropod mob! You blubbery, rubbery, bellyfoot blobs! Can't you see that I'm trying to *save* you!"

Even the bullies were impressed. This was no squidgy little squirt. This was some slug, this was.

"Save us from what?" said an astonished User-Friendly.

"A fate worse than death!" answered Software. "If you don't learn to crawl in straight lines, you'll be SHELLED! WINKLE-PICKED! SLUGIFIED!"

"OOOOOOGHHHHAAAAA!" went all the snails with a shudder.

Even the two bullies looked worried and ready to do as they were told.

The snails watched with bated breath while Software dived into The Hole and whispered something to them both. Eventually, one of them grinned.

"Megabyte," he said. "That suits me just fine."

"Kilowatt," said the other. "That's a name really worf 'aving!"

A moment later, Software emerged from The Hole, flanked proudly by the newly named bullies.

"My personal bodyguards," he boasted.

"WHAAT?" gasped the snails. "Whose side are you supposed to be on?"

"If that doesn't take the biscuit!" said User-Friendly. "What's got into you Software? What are you playing at?"

But Software couldn't tell them of course. A computer stupor is a bit like a hypnotic trance: you don't know you're in one, when you're in one. The only cure is some sort of shock.

"I'm not playing!" said Software. "I'm in deadly earnest! Don't you know what they do to squigglies? They shoot them – ZOOOOOOM! ZAP!"

"But we're not squigglies, we're SNAILS!" said Whizz-Kid.

"You squiggle, just the same," said Software. "Unlike Megabyte here, and his fine friend

Kilowatt. *They* know what rulers are about! *They* know how to crawl straight! They're going to help me square you up!"

"Oh yeah!" said Megabyte and Kilowatt. "And what's in it for us?"

"POWER!" answered Software. "And the most comfortable spot in The Hole! As for you lot –" he said, turning to the rest of the snails, "I bet some of you don't even know your head from your tail, never mind left from right! Now you're going to learn! And remember! One squiggle and you're dead!"

Then, with Megabyte and Kilowatt as his proud and willing henchmen, he marched them all the

way to the family sitting room, until they reached Mr Potter's desk.

Strewn across it was a pile of exercise books that Mr Potter had been marking. "You know what these are –" said Software. "*EXercise books*! For snail *EXercises*!"

The snails gawped at him, boggle-eyed and chinless, too bewildered to say a word.

"B-b-but –" tried Whole-Meal.

"OFF WITH HIS SHELL!" shouted Software, so that not a snail dared to say any more. Along the edges they went, up and down the margins, on the lines, between the lines, trying for dear life to crawl straight.

By morning they were getting quite good. When the Potter family began to stir and they had to leave off, Software insisted that they should practise some more on the front doorstep before returning to The Hole, to see what they could do without guidelines. Any snail that went off on a squiggle was bumped and jostled into line by Megabyte and Kilowatt, who were already looking just like their names.

Soon the doorstep was criss-crossed with slime trails, which made a network of triangles and squares.

Only User-Friendly noticed that two of the snails had missed their training. Slipper-Sock had smelt a sultana amongst the Christmas decorations and decided to hunt for it. As for poor old Cat-Flap, she had stayed in a huff inside her shell. Bellyfoot blob indeed! She'd never been so insulted in her life!

User-Friendly heaved a big sigh. Either Software was up to something, or else he'd gone squiggly in the head!

Chapter 9

Something Strange Afoot

It soon became clear the next morning that Software wasn't the only one to be obsessed with straight lines.

So was Betsy Potter.

When she didn't appear for breakfast, Tom was sent to wake her up.

Betsy was already dressed, but she had strangely staring eyes and a vacant expression on her face. The computer was still switched on.

"Betsy!" stormed Tom. "Have you had my computer on all night –?"

Betsy looked straight past him. With the jerkiness of a robot, she made her way stiffly downstairs.

First she set about re-arranging the cereal packets in a straight line on the table.

Then she started on the cutlery.

Next she went about the room, straightening pictures, cushions, chairs, finally trying with vexation to rid the cat of the curl in its tail.

"Stop fooling Betsy!" said her father.

"Sit down and eat your breakfast!" said her mother.

Like a robot under remote control, Betsy did as she was told. "Zoooooom!" she went, lifting a spoonful of cornflakes. "Zap!" as it went into her mouth.

"Stop acting like a zombie!" her mother scolded.

"She had my computer on all n –" began Tom.

"NO TIME TO TALK!" went his parents.

Things were no better at school. Mr Potter's first lesson happened to be with Betsy's class. When he gave out the books he had marked, there were howls of disgust from the children.

"Sir. Ooooogh! Oh sir!"

"Eeeaaaaawgh! Sirrrrrr! What's this?"

"My book's all slimy sir!"

"And mine's stuck round the edges!"

Mr Potter was trying to work out what had happened when Betsy strode out to the front.

"WELL?" said Mr Potter.

"I've got a complaint to make."

"You're not the only one."

"These lines on our exercise books –"

"Y-e-e-e-s," went Mr Potter, nearly choking through clenched teeth. "What do you know about them?"

"They're DISGRACEFUL!" Betsy declared. "They're squiggly as well as slimy. Couldn't you have used a ruler? Couldn't you have made them straight?"

Mr Potter groaned and buried his head in his hands.

At home, Mrs Potter worried about her daughter as she got stuck into the housework. Betsy had certainly been in a very strange mood that morning. Perhaps it was some sort of protest, something to do with her petition.

"It's all my fault," thought Mrs Potter. "I don't set the right sort of example. After all, I am a housewife. I cook. I wash. I clean. Even worse, I *like* it. But it's no good. I must get out of my cosy little shell and go into the cold cruel world. I must get myself a job."

She was picking up the milk from the doorstep when she noticed something very strange. It was covered in slimy trails. Not the usual, squiggly mazes, but trails in neat straight lines. Criss-crossing over each other, they made a network of triangles and squares.

"It's that slug!" thought Mrs Potter jubilantly. "He's up to his tricks again! Whatever can it mean? He's certainly changed his style. These aren't artistic trails. These are geometric! As if – as if –!"

And she remembered Betsy that morning, with her stiff, angular movements, straightening everything out. Very mysterious!

Mrs Potter pondered. Perhaps it was a warning of some sort – a warning about the weather? Or was it something more serious – that hole in the ozone layer? Or sinister aliens at work?

Forgetting all about the housework Mrs Potter made a drawing of the trails and compared it with the other 'Snail-Trail-Diagrams-And-Data' she already had filed away. "It's a good job I'm at home to keep an eye on things," she said to herself. "Something strange is afoot and I intend to find out what it is!"

But how to set about it?

She must catch some slugs and snails! Or better still – Superslug himself!

Chapter 10

A Packet of Dipity

"Come and share my sultana," said Slipper-Sock that evening to Cat-Flap, who was still inside her shell.

Cat-Flap didn't need asking twice. First, because she was starving. Secondly, because she preferred a sultana any day to square-bashing with the rest of the snails. And the nonsense Software kept spouting! What had she heard him say?

"Straight lines are superior to squiggles.

Slugs can do straight lines.

Therefore slugs are superior."

He'd even told the snails to put the ruler back upright, and declared it was a totem pole!

Yes, she much preferred a sultana.

Slowly, Cat-Flap began to come out of her shell, first one tentacle, then the other, before the rest of her appeared. She had just reached the cellar through the air vent when she was joined by User-Friendly, who had also had enough square-bashing and had managed to give the others the slip this time.

"Did someone mention sultanas?" he asked.

So the three snails settled down together, in the box of Christmas decorations, to chew over the single sultana that Slipper-Sock had found at last, to chew over their problems.

"Do you know," said User-Friendly, "it was Software himself who once told me that snails were meant to squiggle. He said it gave them lots of – what was that funny word – *serendipity.*"

"Serendipity," agreed Cat-Flap, though she had no idea what it meant.

The trio of snails nodded wisely, as if they couldn't agree more. There was a pause before Slipper-Sock asked, "What *is* serendipity?"

"It's a way of making happy and unexpected discoveries by accident," said User-Friendly. "You don't have it if you go in straight lines."

"There's some of that in here!" exclaimed Slipper-Sock.

"Some of what?" asked User-Friendly.

"That dipity stuff," said Slipper-Sock proudly. "I found a whole packet of it amongst the Christmas decorations."

"Don't be silly!" said User-Friendly. "Serendipity is the way things happen. An accidental way. It doesn't come in packets."

"It does, so there!" protested Slipper-Sock. "I'll show you!" and he burrowed around for a while before turning up a cellophane packet.

"That's not serendipity!" said User-Friendly. "That's glitter. Gold and silver glitter!"

"It's also a happy and unexpected discovery," said Slipper-Sock, looking crestfallen.

For a while the three snails fell silent.

"Whoever would have thought it of Software," sighed User-Friendly at last.

"You know," said Cat-Flap, chewing thoughtfully, "I think it's because he feels unloved. He's unhappy at being a slug. What he needs is cusses and kiddles."

"Kisses and cuddles," corrected User-Friendly.

"Lots of hugs," said Slipper-Sock.

"We need to make Software feel *pleased* to be a slug," said User-Friendly. "We need to make him feel special."

Then he had a thought that made him suddenly very excited.

"Slipper-Sock! You're right! You *have* got serendipity! Oodles and oodles of it! Listen. Where's that packet?" and he outlined to the two snails the most amazing and audacious plan.

"We'll never do it," gasped Cat-Flap when he had finished. "Not with that Megabyte and Kilowatt around."

They had eaten the sultana and were sinking once more into despair when they heard something really extraordinary.

"SLUGGLES!" called a voice. "ICKY-WICKY SLUGLETS."

The snails crinkled up in amazement.

"SNAILYCHOPS!" went the voice. "SQUIGGLY-WIGGLY-WRIGGLIES!'"

The snails raced to the top of The Hole and peeped through the gap below the sink.

There stood Mrs Potter on the doorstep, peering across the drive. In one hand she held a torch, in the other a punnet of ... of ... the snails sniffed very hard ... STRAWBERRIES!

"SLIMY-WIMEY SNAILIES!" she called, putting it down and closing the door.

"Do you know," said User-Friendly in disbelief, "I think she means US!"

All thoughts of serendipity vanished from their minds, to be replaced by the thought of strawberries. They climbed out of The Hole and made their way cautiously towards the punnet.

But someone else had got there first: Megabyte and Kilowatt. At the first whiff they'd deserted

Software in the garden and gone straight to it. Greedily they sucked and slurped.

"I thought it was too good to be true," said User-Friendly, gulping back his disappointment. "Never mind, now these two are occupied, we can carry out our plan. Back to the Christmas box, Slipper-Sock. We'll be needing that packet of dipity."

Although they did not know it, it was a happy and unexpected turn of events for them, for a hedgehog lurked in the shadows. He too had smelt the strawberries. He had also seen the two great snails. Snail and strawberry mash! He couldn't believe his luck!

But just as he charged, Mrs Potter opened the door.

"Caught you!" she crowed, and scooped the lot up from under his nose.

Chapter 11

Glitterslime

In the garden the snails were hard at work and Software, still in his stupor, was bossing them about on his own.

"Remember, one squiggle and you're dead," he kept saying.

The snails knew just what he meant, as they edged fearfully along the washing line, trying not to look down.

"Can we try the garden line next?" they asked. They didn't dare mention that it was much lower down, above soft earth and a sowing of peas. They felt Software wouldn't approve. He was just about to answer when User-Friendly and the two others appeared below.

"A-one. A-two. A-one two three!" went Cat-Flap and the three of them sang in chorus:

"If you want to make him happy
Hug a slug.
If you want to make him happy
Hug a slug.
You can hug him any time
Say you love him for his slime
If you want to make him happy
Hug a slug!"

The other snails listened in amazement, their concentration squiggling like mad. At the start of the second verse, they just couldn't help joining in:

"If you want to make him happy
Hug a slug
If you want to make him happy
Hug a slug.
Say you love him just as well
Though he hasn't got a shell
If you want to make him happy
Hug a slug!"

– they sang precariously from the washing line.

Talk about surprised! Software was completely frazzled! Software was all but crunckled!

"Megabyte! Kilowatt!" he called out feebly, but of course they were nowhere to be seen.

Then, as if they had never been so pleased to see anyone in their lives, the snails all crowded round Software, an adoring, suffocating mob.

"I must CRAWL and THINK very straight," he said to himself, trying to remain level-headed, and managing to get out of their way. He hadn't got far when a voice called out, "Software! Just look at your slime. It isn't just straight, it's … it's … GLITTERY!"

Software looked behind him. Sure enough, his trail sparkled and shone in the moonlight.

"Good gracious!" exclaimed Slipper-Sock. "Glitterslime!"

"A miracle!" said Cat-Flap.

"Wondrous!" said User-Friendly.

Software doubled back on his tracks, blinking in disbelief as he inspected the gold and silver trail. Following closely all the way went Slipper-Sock and Cat-Flap, sprinkling from the packet held between them. Soon Software was covered in glitter. The rest of the snails gathered round, most of them truly in awe.

"What a fabulous slug!"

"A mythical slug!"

"A most miraculous slug!"

Software was so bewildered that he kept trying to crawl away, from himself, from the glittering slime. This way he went, and that, squirming, wriggling, squiggling, with the admiring snails trailing after. They got nearer and nearer to The Hole.

None of them noticed the strange dark shape in the shadows. It was the hedgehog, in a furious temper.

But here was his second chance. All that lovely food, all those tasty morsels, just waiting to be gobbled up.

With a snort, the hedgehog rushed upon them.

Chapter 12

Ruses and Rules

The hedgehog got a terrible shock. He'd never seen snails move so fast! As straight as the spokes of a wheel they raced for cover under the stone sink.

The only thing left was a peculiar looking slug. Snatching him up in his jaws, the hedgehog spat him straight out in disgust. He didn't want glitterslug snack!

Cheated for a second time, by now he was really mad. The snails watched in terror as he sniffed all round the gap between the stone sink and the top of The Hole, trying to find a way in. They could see his long wet snout and the glimpse of a greedy eye.

"Don't worry," said User-Friendly. "He'll never make it with all those prickles."

But User-Friendly had spoken too soon. One second later, the hedgehog squeezed between two bricks and landed with a thud in their midst.

Another second after that and a very dazed Software appeared.

"What happened?" he said. "Where am I?"

Jolted by his narrow escape, he was out of his computer stupor.

Although of course she didn't know it, Betsy was still in hers. No one else knew it either, though they did know one thing for sure: something strange had come over Betsy Potter!

And they knew something else: the something strange had caught on!

Ever since the confrontation with her father over the slime trails, Betsy had been the star of the school. She'd done it with such nerve! She hadn't batted an eyelid! Now, as far as the girls were concerned, Betsy could do no wrong. In fact, whatever she did was right.

On Tuesday, when Betsy spent the playtimes and dinnertimes tightrope walking along the white lines that marked out the football pitch, the rest of the girls did the same.

On Wednesday, in art, when she insisted on drawing her picture with a ruler, the rest of the girls followed suit.

As for the vacant expression on her face – it was easy enough to copy. And as for walking around like clockwork – it became the latest craze.

It was like an amazing game of 'Follow my

Leader'. The girls found it wonderful fun.

Mr Potter did not.

Nor did he know what to do.

After all, they weren't breaking any rules!

By Thursday, Mr Potter had had enough. If he was like a cardboard cut-out headmaster, they were like paper-cut girls. Copy-cat, paper-chain girls! And it was Betsy who started it all. Betsy! His very own daughter! Making him look such a fool!

Why? What was she up to?

It was then that Mr Potter tumbled to it. Of course! It was all some sort of protest, to do with that petition of theirs. Sly little monkeys! Clever little devils! Why hadn't he realized before?

He had to do something about it. On Friday, Mr Scroggles would be back. It was no good asking Mrs Potter to help. He could guess whose side she would be on. Besides, she was mysteriously busy on some project of her own. He would have to tackle Betsy by himself. He did so on Thursday evening.

"I know just what you're up to my girl," he said, "and if you think this little ruse of yours is going to work, you're very much mistaken."

"Ruse? What's a ruse?" asked Betsy blankly.

"This silly act of yours! This wall-eyed zombie stuff! I didn't drop off a Christmas tree you know. I'm not going to fall for that!"

"Act?" said Betsy. "I don't know what you mean."

Tom sighed and rolled his eyes up to the ceiling. He thought his dad's act was much worse than Betsy's.

"So none of that nonsense tomorrow."

"No Dad."

"Mr Scroggles will be back."

"Yes Dad."

"I want him to see that I've done a good job."

"Of course Dad."

"STOP THAT!"

"Yes Dad."

At this point Mr Potter lost his temper and stormed out of the room. Tom went after him.

"You know Dad, I don't think Betsy *is* putting anything on. She's been sort of odd ever since she borrowed my computer. She had it on all night long. Do you think it might have hypnotized her? Put her in a trance or something? She seems to look straight *through* everything."

Mr Potter turned on him angrily. "I know just what this is my lad. It's another ruse so that you don't have to lend it to her again. Well, it isn't going to work. Can't you see I'm a busy man? I've had enough of the pair of you!"

Chapter 13

Prickles in a Pickle

Software had come out of his stupor to find that he was, and wasn't a hero.

"Thank goodness you taught us straight lines," Whizz-Kid said to him. "If we'd squiggled in our usual way, we wouldn't have got away."

"But what shall we do about *him*?" said Whole-Meal. "It's all your fault Software. You got us into this."

For two days and nights now the hedgehog had been trapped in The Hole. It had soon become clear from the way he scratched at corners and sniffed at cracks, that there was no way he could get out.

From their upside-down position beneath the stone sink, the snails watched him with increasing despair. What use were his prickles to him now? What dread in his terrible jaws?

By Friday the whimpering and scampering had stopped and the hedgehog had become very still.

"He'll die if he doesn't get out soon," said Cat-Flap.

"Not if one of us drops in every so often," said Slipper-Sock.

"After you," said Floppy-Disc.

"I wish he *would* die," said Fast-Forward heartlessly. "I want to get back into our Hole."

"Well I'm not sharing it with *any* sort of hedgehog," said User-Friendly. "Dead or alive."

Software hadn't said much. Although he had snapped out of his stupor, he was still very confused, unable to work out what had really happened, and what he'd only imagined. The hedgehog was real enough, curled up into a frightened ball.

"Poor old hedgehog," he sighed.

"What do you mean?" said Fast-Forward. "He's a horrible old hedgehog. He'd eat us all up if he could."

"He can't help it," said Software. "It's just the way he's made."

"And what about the way *you're* made?" said Cat-Flap indignantly. "Always wanting to be different, always wishing for a shell."

"And what about the way *we're* made," added Floppy-Disc. "Squiggling isn't just a pastime. It's a way of life."

"Of course it is," said Software. "It gives you lots of . . . what's that funny word . . . serendipity."

"You WHAT!" protested the snails, spluttering fit to burst, "Do you mean to say –

"After all –"

"What about –?"

"Cheek!"

"What about that totem pole?" User-Friendly managed to say.

Software looked down at the ruler, as if for the very first time. Something seemed to click in his brain.

"How did *that* get here?" he asked.

"You tell us," said the snails.

"We've got to get it *out*," said Software urgently. "No wonder this dreadful thing has happened. It's all because of that ruler. It's a monstrosity! Such things are *anathema* to gastropods!"

"A whatima?" asked Slipper-Sock.

"A curse! A spell! A bad sign!" went Software. "Anti-slug! Anti-snail! Anti-squiggle! Why – squiggles are the *essence* of snails!"

"But how can we get it out with that hedgehog lying in wait?" asked User-Friendly.

"Don't worry about him," said Software. "He's too weak to hurt a fly."

Then Software set about organizing the snails, some as guides, some as rollers, some as levers, to push, to shove the ruler up and out of The Hole. It was very hard work.

"What we need," said Software, huffing and

puffing as he directed the operation, "is a couple of big, burly, hefty fellows –"

"– like Megabyte and Kilowatt –?" interrupted Fast-Forward ... and the memory came flooding back to Software, of two great armour-plated snails, descended from a racing snail. Where on earth had they got to?

None of the snails seemed to know.

Inside the house, Mrs Potter held two great snails and was putting them through their paces. The discovery of more geometric slime trails around the house had convinced her even further; whatever had got into the snails had also got into Betsy. What she needed was proof.

"Whose a pretty boy then?" she said to Megabyte, holding a slice of cucumber under his nose to coax him out of his shell.

"Tickytickyticky," she said to Kilowatt, trying to tickle his scaly chin.

"Drat!" she said when the phone rang.

It was Mr Potter on the end of the line. He was talking about Betsy and sounded very distraught.

"What? She's not really?" answered Mrs Potter. "They've walked out of lessons you say? *All* the girls? Like zombies? And Betsy's the ringleader? When will Mr Scroggles be back? Don't worry. I'll be right over."

She was about to leave the house when she noticed the two straight trails. Her snails had almost escaped.

"Oh no you don't," she said, putting them back in their box. "You two are coming with me. There's more to this than meets the eye."

Chapter 14

Old Acquaintance

Mrs Potter didn't go straight to the school. She had just stepped into the drive when the strangest sight caught her eye. It was a ruler, slowly but surely, rising from the hole beneath the stone sink by the doorstep.

Mrs Potter gaped, dropping to her knees, unable to believe what she saw.

Yes! It was Tom's new ruler! The one that had been missing all week!

Up and up it rose, waving and wagging about, before collapsing with a clatter on the gravel. It seemed to have walked by itself.

Or had it? There was only one way to find out.

Mrs Potter went down into the cobwebby cellar and forced open the air vent into The Hole, which was under the stone sink. There she found the hedgehog, huddled into a prickly ball.

"Oh you poor thing," she said, gently lifting him out. Then she took him outside and put him safely in a clump of bushes.

But the mystery still wasn't solved. Could the hedgehog have moved the ruler? It didn't seem

very likely. So what had? Mrs Potter had her suspicions.

On returning to the cellar, she saw that she was right. Clinging to the underside of the stone sink were lots and lots of snails. Amongst them she found a slug – a slug with traces of glitter, a slug she was sure she recognized.

"Why, if it isn't my old friend Superslug," said Mrs Potter. "I thought you might be behind all this! I've been looking everywhere for you. I hope you won't mind, but I'm taking you on an outing. I might be needing your help. Don't worry, you won't be lonely," and she popped him in the box with the snails.

Software was horribly surprised. He was suddenly in suffocating darkness, in a cramped and snaily place.

"Well, well, well. Look wot we've got for company," sneered a voice that sounded all too familiar.

"If it ain't our old friend Software," leered another.

Software blinked in the gloom. These were the

two snails who had called him a squidgy little squirt, who had frightened him nearly to death. But they were just like another two snails, whose names were Megabyte and Kilowatt. *They* hadn't frightened him at all. *They'd* been his personal bodyguards.

Realization slowly dawned. They were one and the same pair of snails. How on earth had that come about?

"Hello … er … fancy meeting you here," he croaked feebly.

The snails pushed their scaly faces close to his.

"You'd better fancy a way out of 'ere or it will be very much the worse for you," they snarled.

"I w-w-will. D-don't p-panic. K-keep c-calm" stammered Software in a jitter. "J-j-just d-d-do eggs-eggs-exactly as I tell you and ever-everything will be all-all right."

Mrs Potter arrived at the school at the same time as Mr Scroggles. When Mr Potter saw them together, he wished his shoes would swallow him up.

The last time his wife had been to the school, she'd been covered in snail slime. This time it was cobwebs.

"Er . . . Mr Scroggles . . . I believe you've met my . . . er wife."

"And how have you managed Potter?" said Mr Scroggles warmly.

"Er . . . well . . . just a little problem with the girls. Some kind of silly protest." He didn't dare tell him that all the girls had abandoned the classrooms and were out on the football pitch, following Betsy round the edges. The other teachers were doing their best to bring them in, while the boys were just enjoying it all.

Luckily, Mr Scroggles didn't ask further. He was too full of his own news.

"Marvellous course I've been on Potter. All about sexism in schools. Run by this wonderful headmistress. Do you realize I'm thirty years out of date? You younger members of staff should have been keeping me up with the changing times. All that nonsense about girls being girls and boys being boys. It's finished! It's over! From now on –"

But before Mr Scroggles had time to say more, a worried teacher came into the room.

"Mr Potter! Quickly! You'd better come!"

The four of them rushed into the playground. The girls had left the football pitch and followed Betsy to the very high wall that ran all round the playground. They had followed so far, but no further. Betsy walked like a robot along the top, fearlessly looking ahead, not a footstep out of place. "ZOOOOOOOOOOOOOOOOM!" she went and "ZAP!"

"Cor! Look at that!" said the boys.

"Blimey! What a nerve!"

"Betsy!" said Mr and Mrs Potter together in alarm.

At the sound of her name, Betsy lost her balance.

"WATCH OUT!" she yelled at Mr Scroggles. "Remember, one squiggle and you're dead!"

And then she fell off the wall.

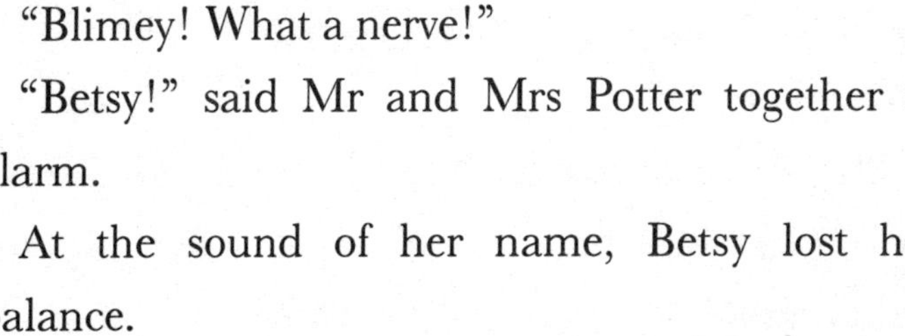

Chapter 15

Footloose and Fancy Free

Fortunately, Betsy wasn't hurt, just shocked right out of her stupor. "What happened?" she said. "Where am I?"

After a drink and a biscuit in the headmaster's study, she was her old self again. But no, she didn't know why she had walked on the wall. In fact, she couldn't remember anything much since borrowing Tom's computer.

Then Mrs Potter told them about the curious discovery she had made about the slime trails, and that she felt there was some kind of connection.

Mr Scroggles listened politely. Tom and Mr Potter winced with embarrassment.

Another shock was on its way. Mr Scroggles told

all the children to assemble in the hall because he had an announcement to make. "Times have changed over the years," he said, "but I've been too busy running the school to notice. I've heard about your petition. From now on, girls and boys are to have exactly the same lessons."

A loud cheer went up amongst the girls. "Hooray for Mr Scroggles! Hooray for Betsy Potter!"

Then Mr Scroggles spoke again. He said that Mrs Potter had a keen interest in local natural history and that she would be running a new wildlife club for the school. "If you clear a space right now," he said, "I believe she has something to show you."

Mrs Potter took two very large snails out of a box and placed them on the floor.

"I call this one Posy," she said, "and this other one Blossom. Now watch!"

The two snails had been warned by Software. They had only one hope of escape: straight lines! triangles! squares!

Off they set together, in swift, straight lines, so that the children turned it into a race. "Come on Blossom," yelled one half, while "Keep going Posy!" yelled the other.

Posy won and Blossom was furious. Just to go one better, he went off on a pattern of squares. Not to be outdone, Posy did triangles inside them; then they zig-zagged in diamond shapes together.

"Cor!" said the children.

"Remarkable!" said Mr Scroggles.

"You ain't seen nothing yet," said Mrs Potter, taking out Software with a flourish. "This slug here is a genius. He's Pythagoras compared to the others," and she set him down on the floor.

The children waited in silence.

Software did nothing for a while, then he began to squiggle.

Untidily, he wriggled.

Slimily, he scribbled.

Mrs Potter's face fell.

"OOOOOOOOOGHAAAAAA!" went the children.

"He seems to be a common garden slug," said Mr Scroggles.

"I must have picked up the wrong one," said Mrs Potter. "But I'm sure … I could have sworn …"

"It doesn't matter what sort of slug he is," said Betsy, picking him up and putting him back in his box. "He can't help the way he's made. He doesn't like being on show."

And it was agreed that since Posy and Blossom obviously loved being on show, they should stay in the school as mascots, while Software should be taken home.

Before they left, Mr Scroggles spoke to Mr Potter. "You look as if you've been under a bit of a strain this week. You should take up knitting. It's wonderfully soothing for nerves. Just look what I knitted at the conference this week," and he proudly displayed his yellow socks.

That evening, Tom found Betsy in her room, looking very forlorn.

"What's the matter with you?" he asked – but Betsy had no need to tell him. All her dolls and cuddly toys were piled up in the middle of the room. All her mouse posters had come down.

"Look," said Tom kindly, "if Dad can keep his old teddy bear – I don't see why you can't keep those." He paused and added bashfully, "I'd never part with Bunnyflumkin."

Betsy looked a bit brighter.

"And in any case," Tom continued, "you've made your point. You've got your own way. But tell me. *Was* it a ruse? Were you putting it on all the time?"

"Putting what on?" asked Betsy, with wide-eyed, exaggerated innocence.

"Software," said User-Friendly that same evening, "you got rid of those two great bullies. You got rid of the ruler and the hedgehog, all in such a roundabout way. Was it just a happy and unexpected turn of events, or brilliant squiggly thinking?"

"I wish I knew," sighed Software. "Tell me if you ever find out."

After that, whenever Software was in earshot,

the snails remembered to complain loudly about their shells:

"Such a burden!"

"Suffocating!"

"Slugs have all the luck."

"Only slugs can travel light."

"Nothing to lug about on their backs."

– which didn't fool Software one bit! No, he'd made up his own mind. He didn't want a shell after all. They weren't all they were cracked up to be. They weren't as good as prickles, which were sometimes no good at all.

"It's lovely to be meeeeee
Footloose and fancy freeeeee."

– he would sing to himself. And then he would stop to ask himself a question: Pythagoras! Who was Pythagoras? One day he must find out.

As for Mr Potter, he'd decided that he wasn't cut out to be a headmaster. Now he sits in a comfortable armchair, and if you listen carefully you'll hear him saying to himself, "Knit, purl, knit, purl, knit two together, pull wool forward, knit, purl . . ."

Yes, he's taken up knitting!

The Story Behind the Story

A slug is a very unlikely hero for a story. Even to mention them seems impolite. So why choose to write about one?

The answer is – I didn't. This creepy-crawly chose me. The Software Superslug stories really did begin with mystery slime trails in our sitting room.

We were very intrigued, for these slime trails looked intelligent. What's more, they all led to the pouffe.

A night's vigil revealed the truth – that the culprit wasn't a snail as we supposed, but a slug. Our reaction was OOOOAAAAGHH!

But there was something so dignified and determined about the creature, despite our human disapproval, that we decided to live and let live. It was out of this that the stories grew.

Perhaps we shouldn't admit it – but there are still tell-tale trails every night. I guess we're stuck with them, as we can't help wondering what they will lead to next.

Joyce and James Dunbar have written and illustrated several other stories together. They live with their two children in Stratford-on-Avon.